Copyright © 2012 Neil Cutler
www.neilcutler.com

All rights reserved.
No part of this publication may be
reproduced or transmitted in any
form or by any means, electronic
or mechanical, including photocopy,
recording or any information storage
and retrieval system, without prior
permission in writing from the
copyright owner.

Distributed by Index Book SL
Consell de Cent, 160 Local 3
08015 Barcelona
T +34 93 454 5547
ib@indexbook.com
www.indexbook.com

ISBN: 978-84-15308-13-3

Printed in China

DESIGNER, LEAVES ENGLAND, GOES TO BARCELONA...

The designs of Neil Cutler

HOLA!

Ok, I admit that that's about as much as I could say when I first arrived in Barcelona in 1987, having left England two years earlier and having been on the road, so to speak, since then. My arrival in October of that year with a folder of work under my arm wasn't really part of any great plan, but I was soon up and running in this great Mediterranean city, the city that I now call home.

I was brought up in Northern England, and like most potential designers, I loved drawing and painting as a kid. It wasn't until years later, having completed a foundation art course that I was pointed in the direction of graphic design, and a degree course at Manchester Polytechnic. During that time I became aware of a design group called Pentagram and in particular one of their former partners, Bob Gill, via a book of his, 'Forget all the rules you ever learned about graphic design'. That was a groovy title for someone studying design!

What it came down to was that these guys had a way of working which seemed like a lot of fun. A lot of their design solutions were like little visual jokes. Ideas. It opened my eyes to a way of thinking, basically that thinking in design was more important than just doing. It involved solving problems with visual ideas, telling a story, being witty, making people smile, but above all communicating something via a unique solution. Design could be exciting. And good ideas could be timeless. It's where it's at for me, and it is the way I've worked ever since. 'Forget all the rules...' still sits proudly on my bookshelf today.

Around the same time I came across another Gill, Eric (no relation to Bob), designer of the typeface Gill Sans. For some obscure reason I'd decided to do my design degree thesis on gravestones and I found myself rummaging around cemeteries in London, making rubbings of Gill's exquisite hand lettering carved in stone, unaware of how frequently I would be using his sans serif typeface in the future (over twenty designs in this book, including the cover title, use Gill Sans in some shape or form). So a nod to Eric and Bob then.

Design degree accomplished, a friend from the course and I flew to New York with our rucksacks full of nothing much and a box of slides of our work, and travelled all over the States. With just enough money for beer and gas, we hitchhiked and drove from east to west and north to south and back again. Work offers came, but the object of the trip was to see some of the world and we headed back to London to kick-start our careers.

My London experience came to an abrupt end two years later when I went off to Andorra for my first ever ski trip and promptly fell down the slopes and head over heels for our ski instructress. One thing led to another and a few months later, with the next ski season looming, I left my job in London and headed back to Andorra for the winter. Not the smartest career move, but my skiing improved no end.

Barcelona was only 130km down the road from Andorra, but with the skiing season over there was still some travelling to do, and we spent the next 12 months driving around Australia in a van! I spent half of that time working as a designer in Sydney, Melbourne and Perth, which aside from being a great work experience, kept us going for the whole year. It was the trip of a lifetime and the travel diary notebooks I made during the journey are featured later in this book.

Once back in Europe, and having recently been awarded the '92 Olympic Games, Barcelona seemed like the natural choice for the next move. So following a brief stint back at my old job in London, we headed to Spain.

This bustling Mediterranean port city was a huge contrast to the vast open spaces of Australia where I'd just spent the last year.

But the sun was shining here too. And there was a creative buzz in Barcelona.

Within a week of arriving I was freelancing at one of the top design studios of the time. Unclear about just how long this next phase of my life was going to last, I never took Spanish classes, picking it up as I went along, hanging on to the theory that designing depended more on my artistic skills than my linguistic ones.

But Barcelona, Catalonia and Spain had captivated me. It's people, their wonderful sense of modesty, the chaos and spontaneity, improvisation, their 'savoir vivre'. Before realising it, I'd become sort of established in Barcelona and within a few years had my own studio, with clients that were happy with my work and that I was happy to work for.

To this day I still work on a freelance basis (it's a great word freelance, sounds like freedom). Occasionally someone will say 'I recognise your style' and this often baffles me. Maybe it's because I illustrate my own logos, or comes from the influence that the sun has undoubtedly had on my use of colour. Or the typefaces I use, that tend to be traditional (Gill Sans included) rather than trendy. Or the fact that I avoid imitation script lettering (easy to spot as repeat letters are always the same) and where necessary commission calligraphy.

Or maybe it's just that way of thinking again. Whatever, if I really do have a style, I like to think that its because its hard to discern between the older and newer designs. Good design should, after all, transcend fashion.

I often think its funny that in a country where eating and drinking is a national pastime, so much of the work I have done in Spain has revolved around designs for restaurants and food packaging. And although some of the designs have won awards, I think it's fair to say that I get more satisfaction from coming across one of my beer cans tossed by the roadside, fading under the midday sun, or from knowing that someone stole the menu from one of the restaurants I've worked on, just because they liked the design.

There's no particular order to this book, basically because my working day is like that- the work of a designer doesn't really come in chapters.
A typical day will find me flipping from one project to the next, taking a brief and coming up with solutions for logos, packs, identities and restaurants…and other bits and pieces done as the other 'freelancer', the 'free for friends' one, often the nicest jobs to work on!

Democracy was still in its infancy when I arrived in the Catalan capital. On the Ramblas selling caged birds was still the norm, as was selling yourself for some at the more seedy end of the boulevard! Bullfighting wasn't even questioned, let alone banned, and you could happily ride around town on your Vespa without a helmet on, or drive home in your Seat Ibiza without a seat belt on (even after a night out).

Often cited as the best ever, the impact the Olympic Games had on Barcelona as a city and a place to visit was immeasurable.
The 'Make Barcelona Beautiful' campaign of the time made Barcelona even more beautiful.
It was the face-lift of all face-lifts. Barcelona was transformed.

But its Mediterranean spirit remains intact. You can still get lost in the myriad of narrow streets of the Barrio Gótico, or stand in wonder beneath any number of Gaudí buildings, including Barcelona's iconic landmark the Sagrada Família, still unfinished! You can still eat patatas bravas in Bar Tomás, or go out till daylight without it appearing strange, or even take the whole month of August for holiday, again without it appearing strange.

And the sun still shines.

The wonderful beaches of the Costa Brava and ski resorts of the Pyrenees are still close by.
It's still possible to ski in the morning and be on the beach in the afternoon. And you can still catch a ferry to the islands. Or watch one of the best football teams in the world. And yes, the electricity still suddenly goes off every now and again…you can't have it all.

There's always something going on in Barcelona- concerts, music, firework displays, dancing in the streets and local 'fiestas'. One of my favourite days in Barcelona is April the 23rd, Sant Jordi (Saint George's day). It's the day that the streets fill with bookstalls, and people selling roses on every corner. It's the day that the guys give a single red rose to their girlfriends or wives, who in return, give them a book.

Who knows, maybe even this one.

Enjoy.

Mont Roig Café
Identity for a popular cafe in Sitges,
a coastal town close to Barcelona.
The first logo I did for a restaurant
and still one of my favourites.

Anae
Albariño wine made from grapes grown around the estuaries of Galicia, a region famous for its fishing industry and exquisite seafood. I've always had a fondness for lighthouses, so this was the perfect opportunity to use one. A popular wine that has out-sold all expectations.

Ciudad Condal
Ciudad Condal is a tapas restaurant close to Plaça Catalunya and hugely popular with locals and tourists alike. Barcelona is often referred to as the 'Ciudad Condal' (county city), hence the colourful montage of Barcelona imagery.

Boyd
Card announcing the birth of Boyd, the son of friends. I just split the name over two sides, to first announce that it was a boy and then let you know his name.

ATTIC
restaurant

Attic
Attic is a top floor restaurant with a splendid terrace overlooking the famous Ramblas boulevard. The idea for the logo came quite quickly, but the client wanted to see more options. Each time I presented something new I noticed that the original idea was still stuck on the back of his office door, and in the end that's the one we went with. Sometimes first ideas really are the best...

The toilet signs for a restaurant can be as interesting and fun as you want them to be, just as long as they're functional! These two symbols were made by simply jumbling up the letters of the Attic logo.

Rincon & Ruiters
Logo designed for the wedding of
Javier Rincon and Mariëlle Ruiters.
He's Spanish and she's Dutch.

Olive Oil
As part of the design, I wanted to incorporate a colourful image depicting the product's Spanish origins (Spain is the biggest olive oil producing country in the world), and commissioned Martin Rigo to paint this atmospheric Mediterranean landscape scene.

Bogatell
Bogatell takes its name from one of the beaches in Barcelona, and was made for the US market, for Brooklyn wine importers Savorian Inc. The label transmits a Mediterranean spirit- the beach, the sea and a sense of adventure. The wine has enjoyed considerable success in America, and shortly after its introduction became the house white of the Four Seasons hotel in Manhatten.

Bogatell can also be enjoyed at a few select restaurants on the Barcelona waterfront.

CENT 111 ONZE
RESTAURANT

Cent Onze
Cent Onze (one hundred and eleven in Catalan) is the restaurant of Le Méridien hotel, located on the Ramblas at number 111. A refined and understated identity reflects the elegant nature of the restaurant, which offers signature cuisine based around seasonal produce selected from the nearby Boqueria market.

Cent Onze Jazz
Design and photography for brochures promoting the bi-monthly programme of live jazz sessions in the restaurant bar.

Pure Malt Scotch Whisky Aged 12 Years

Glen Roost Whisky
Sweeping calligraphy over a bleak landscape sets a dramatic scene for the bottle and container of this twelve-year-old pure malt whisky. The calligraphy was done by Amanda Adams. There are more examples of her exquisite lettering in this book.

Fresh & Ready
Fresh & Ready started out as one shop selling sandwiches, freshly made in the kitchen each morning. I developed the sunrise image to reflect this. A strong identity was needed as the intention was to expand the business. The concept grew and I was eventually involved in the design of some fifteen shops between Barcelona and Madrid, overseeing the identity and designing posters, labels, packaging, brochures and promotional material.

Alex and Martina
Card designed for friends to announce the birth of their twins, Alex and Martina.

Salta
Visual identity and promotional design work for a restaurant specializing in wok cuisine. The customer chooses the ingredients for wok dishes created on the spot. A corporate orange was chosen to emphasize the dynamic nature of the restaurant.

BLACKO SCHOOL

CENTENARY YEAR

CREATIVE REVIEW MARCH 1989

IN BRIEF

Barcelona-based designer Neil Cutler went back to his Lancashire school and ended up knocking up this neat logo to mark the centenary and provide an identity for the future. That sums it up . . .

Dire Straits' guitarist for five years, Hal Lindes, is supplementing his income with a foray into Still Moving Music has taken him on join its six-strong team.

Blacko School Centenary
Logo designed for the centenary celebrations of Blacko school. The image was applied to mugs, t-shirts and notebooks, etc. which were sold locally to help raise funds for the school.

Dried Herbs and Spices

How many times have you been in front of the spice rack and not been able to find the one you're looking for? With that in mind, the design was based around easily recognisable graphic shapes made from each of the products. This also solved the problem of having to include four languages on such a small label.

All the packs in this book with the Consumer or Eroski logo were designed for Basque supermarket chain Eroski, who have stores throughout Spain, and include four Spanish languages (Castilian, Basque, Catalan and Galician) on all of their food packaging.

El Trobador

Named after Verdi's 'Il Trovatore', the graphics for this restaurant take on a musical theme. The diamond shapes of the logo were inspired by the huge black and white floor tiles of the restaurant. The concept has been very successful, and there are now four *El Trobador* restaurants in Barcelona. All the images here are from the first one on Enric Granados street, in my opinion, still the best.

a la notte placida e bella in ciel se
il viso argenteo mostrava lietor
suonar per bere infino allor

Olives
The simple graphic statement of an olive tree inside an olive shape gives a coherent and memorable identity to this range of jars.

El Raval
El Raval is a cosmopolitan neighbourhood in Barcelona, with a lively boulevard at its centre. The label depicts a typical urban scene, set against the silhouette of Tibidabo, backdrop to the city of Barcelona. Like Bogatell, also shown in this book, El Raval was developed for the US market.

Postres Caseros

Traditional desserts

A colourful identity and appetizing lifestyle photography from Becky Lawton combine to give these traditional desserts from Eroski a more modern feel. The range shares shelf space with the packs of market leader Royal, which I'd also designed several years earlier.

La Botiga
The labels of a bottle and a can gave a packaging theme to this award winning logo for La Botiga (store, in Catalan). To complement the identity, fifteen artists were commissioned to make their own interpretations of traditional packs, and these were used to decorate the restaurant.

The re-design for La Botiga, done nine years later, is shown on page 127.

=

Charity T-Shirt
Alongside personalities like film director Bigas Luna and television presenter Andreu Buenafuente, I was asked to design a T-shirt to help raise funds for the human rights awareness charity Artículo 1. The collection was made in collaboration with retail chain Mango and sold in their stores throughout Spain and abroad. The design sold well and helped to raise several thousand euros for the charity.

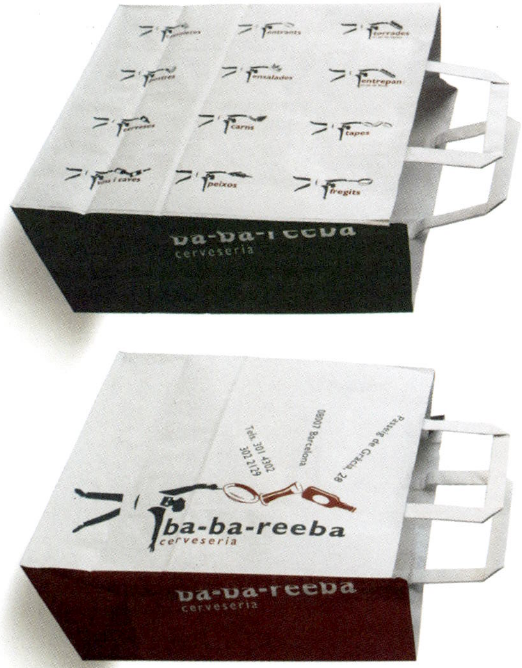

Passeig de Gràcia, 28

08007 Barcelona

Tel. 93 301 4302

Ba-ba-reeba
The name of a restaurant is fundamental to the design of it's identity, so I was a bit thrown off course by this one! All I kept thinking was that it sounded like 'arriba' (above), and in the end that's where the idea for the clever waiters came from.

Si!

Simd!

Simone & Ramón

...zullen gaan trouwen op 12 juni 2003 in Barcelona en je bent/jullie zijn van harte uitgenodigd om dit samen met ons te vieren
...celebrarán su boda el día 12 de junio 2003 en Barcelona y estaríamos encantados de contar con tu/vuestra presencia
...are getting married on the 12th of June 2003 in Barcelona and we'd love you to come and celebrate this day with us

Simone & Ramón
Wedding invitation. Simone says 'sí' (yes) to Ramón.

TE CHOCOLATE & CAFE

 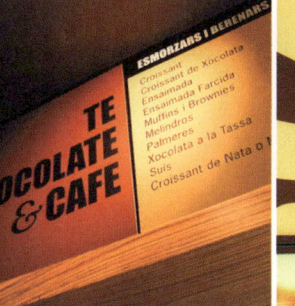 

Te Chocolate & Cafe
Te Chocolate & Cafe is a small cafe (with a long name!) in L'Illa, a popular shopping centre in Barcelona. What to do with such a long name? Turn the problem into the solution and use the words to create the cafe's identity.

Traditional Cheeses
To give a rustic, countryside feel to this design, I commissioned illustrator Jordi Sàbat to produce these two delightful paintings of rural scenes.

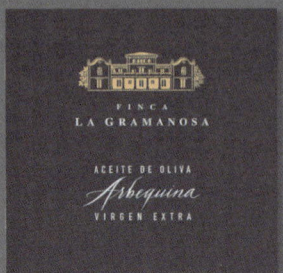

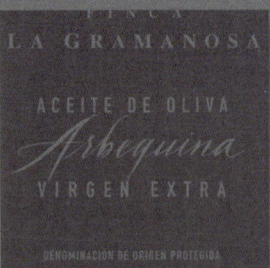

Finca La Gramanosa Olive Oil
Aimed at the gourmet/premium end of the market, this olive oil project took several months to complete and embraced every aspect of the branding process, from the design of the logo and labels, to choosing and printing bottles and capsules. A presentation box and booklet were added to aid sales and add value to the product.

Finca La Gramanosa Wines
The second part of the Finca La Gramanosa project was for wine. By applying the key elements of the olive oil identity, a stylish and elegant image was maintained and a consistent look achieved.

Mango Restaurant
The identity for the restaurant came about by splitting the name in to Man and Go (rather than the more obvious fruit direction). Based on these two simple, direct words, the whole identity was given a sort of African feel.
The first ManGo opened in the centre of Barcelona and the second one on the beachfront.

I still sketch a lot when I'm working on a new job, and these are some of the ideas from the Mango project. It seems I was trying to get something out of 'el mango' (the handle) of a frying pan, before arriving at the Man Go idea.

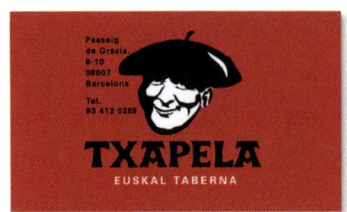

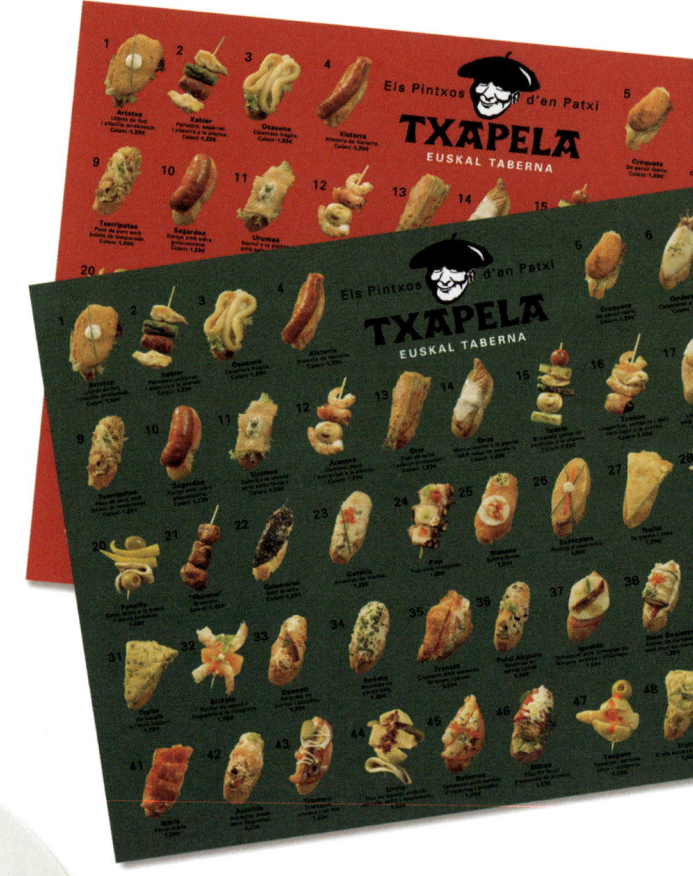

To simplify things for the many tourists who eat in Txapela, the placemats were designed using photos of all the 'pintxos'. This has a double benefit as it also incites people to order more. The placemats have played an important role in the success of the restaurant.

Txapela
Txapela is a successful Basque-style restaurant selling bite-sized 'pintxos'. For the logo I created this likeable character wearing a 'txapela', the typical Basque beret. The red and green colours come from the Basque flag.
Photographer Isabel Azcárate took photos in and around San Sebastian of people wearing 'txapelas' and these were used to decorate the restaurant. There are now two *Txapelas* on Passeig de Gràcia, in the centre of Barcelona.

PastaFina
Branding and packaging design for a range
of fresh pasta and pasta related products,
launched in Tunisia in 2006.

Aurum
Beer consumers are generally very brand loyal, so the aim here was to create a distinctive identity that could compete with the more established beers in the market. The design had to incorporate all the visual language of a beer brand, and at the same time transmit personality and credibility. The successful range extends to a special stronger beer, alcohol-free beer, shandy and flavoured beers. Cheers!

Enero Febrero Marzo Abril Mayo
Junio Julio Agosto Septiembre
Octubre Noviembre Diciembre

ESPAÑA
FRANQUEO PAGADO
P.D.

Calendar Eroski Online

Calendar designed for the online division of Eroski, and given away as a New Year gift to customers. Previous calendars had given more prominence to the background illustration and less to the calendar itself. So I decided to invert the trend and go for a more functional and practical calendar, bold and easy to follow. The problem of colour was solved by filling in the months, Sundays and holidays with details from paintings by Barcelona-based American painter Philip Stanton.

guillén

Un transporte diario que
acerca a las Baleare

Guillén
Guillén is an established transport and logistics company operating between mainland Spain and the Balearic and Canary Islands. Initially formed by several smaller companies, the group merged in 2010 under the Guillén banner. As a major part of the company's activity takes place in ports, a logo incorporating a seagull symbol was developed, representing speed and swiftness, and creating a dynamic and instantly recognisable identity.

ELABORADO EN BOTAS DE ROBLE AMERICANO
A PARTIR DE MOSTOS PROCEDENTES DE
LA VARIEDAD DE UVA PEDRO XIMENEZ

FINO
HEGEMONÍA MAYOR

Manzanilla & Fino
These are two classic, sherry-style wines enjoyed with tapas in the bars and restaurants of Southern Spain. I respected the colour schemes and typographic styles generally used for this type of product, adding lively calligraphy to the *Manzanilla* and a horse to the *Fino*, in homage to the equestrian traditions of Andalucia.

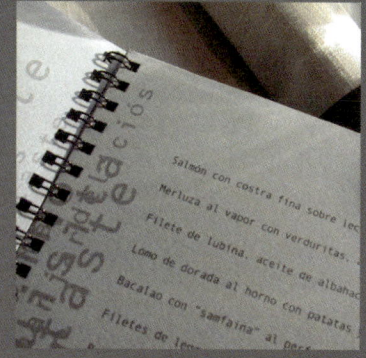  
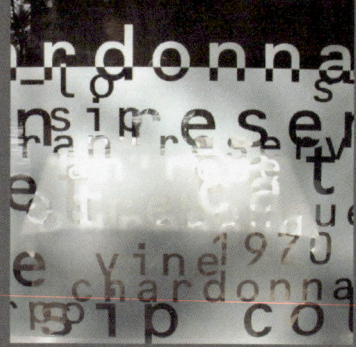  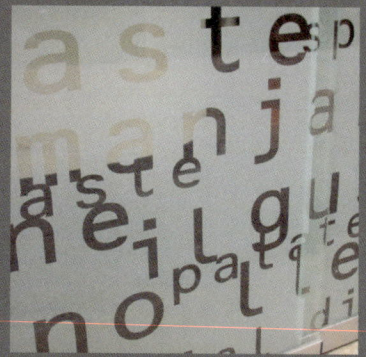

daps
RESTAURANT

Daps
A classy eatery with a façade featuring eight huge windows. The entire identity was built around a potpourri of food and drink related words. Applied to the windows, these became an important part of the external and internal image of the restaurant, creating some interesting typographic effects across the tabletops on sunny days.

chocolate sweet sugar chocolate tric
exquisite extauis extauis shauts sella
sucre emoji tasete
dolc

Repsol Christmas Card
Repsol is a Spanish petrol refining company and one of the largest in the world. For the Christmas card I just flipped their logo round to find Santa Claus.

mengi, mengi
cerveseria, cerveseria

Mengi, Mengi
Not a very interesting name for a restaurant (Eat, Eat, in Catalan), but on the positive side, repetitive and symmetrical. The design solution: an identity that was also repetitive and symmetrical.

Gerbard
Gerbard is a lively little bar in the 'barrio' of Sarrià, where we all get together to watch the Barcelona football games. They organise concerts and events on a regular basis. I designed the logo, placemats and menus... and do posters when needed. All in exchange for beer, wine and tapas! Nice one.

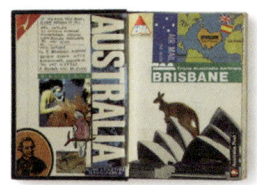 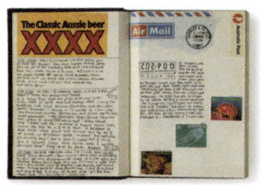 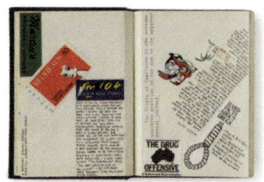 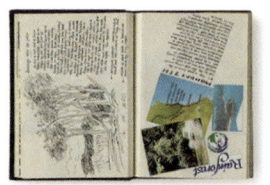

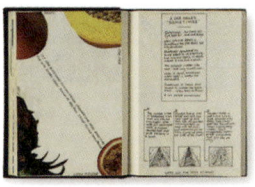 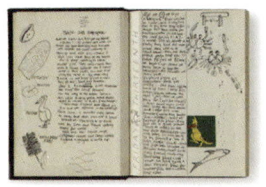 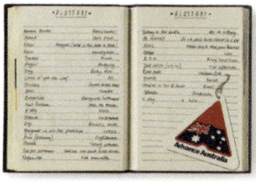 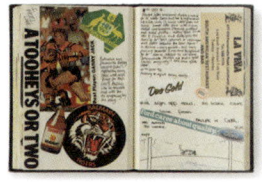

 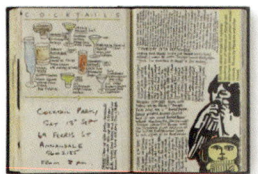  

 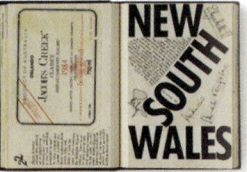  

  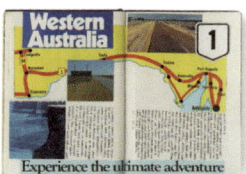 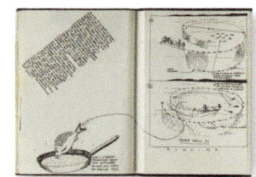

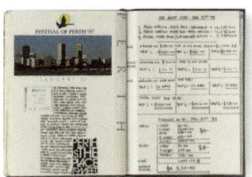   

Sketch books Australia.

Pages from the three travel diary notebooks I made during twelve months on the road in Australia. Notes, sketches and printed paraphernalia of all things Australian.

On the following pages, the rest…

  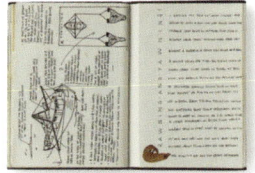

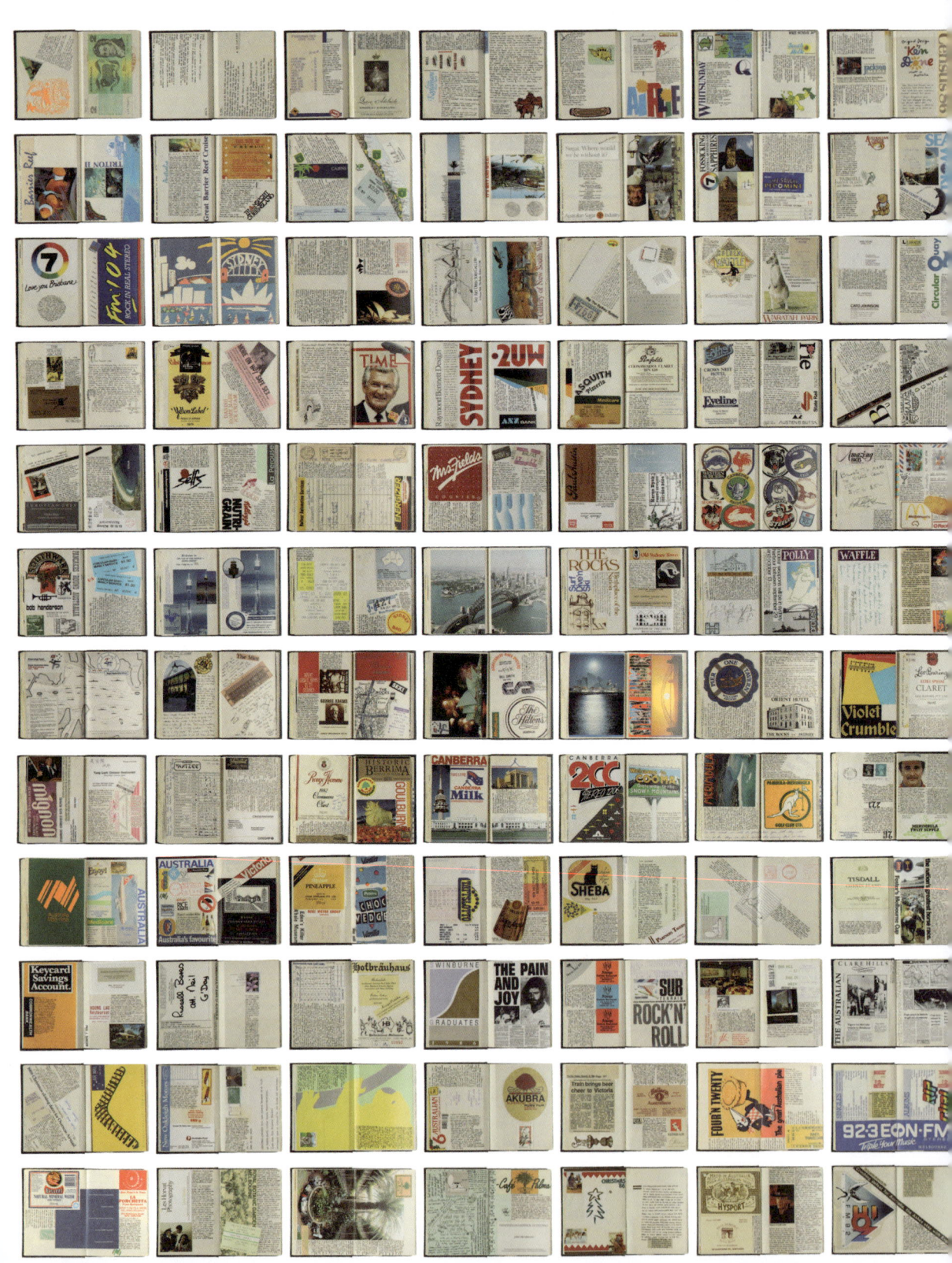

Christmas in London
Card designed to celebrate my first Christmas in London…bus drivers having fun in the snow.

ANDREW5 - W13

Rupert and Pam Andrews have moved
from 53 Eaton Rise W5 to 65 Mattock Lane W13
Telephone 01-579 6768

Moving card
Also designed whilst I was working in London.
A subtle tweak of the 'S' of Andrews was
enough to get the message across.

Héritiers de Vallois Champagne
The brief was to develop an identity for a French champagne, allowing it to compete with the better-known brands in the market. Classical typography and handcrafted calligraphy combine to create an elegant and sophisticated presentation, reflecting all the values and heritage of an established French champagne.

Héritiers de Vallois
Champagne

Ce Champagne doit sa richesse, son équilibre, sa finesse et son arôme authentique à l'habileté traditionnelle avec laquelle il a été élaboré

BRUT

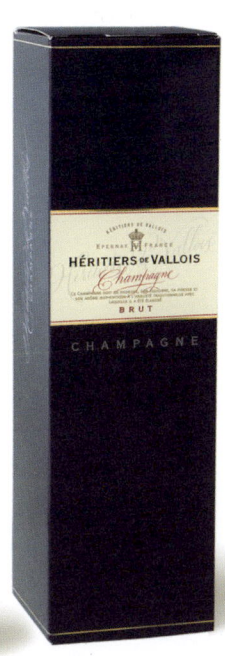

conVoca

Relaciones Públicas
Gabinete de Prensa
Eventos

Convoca
Logo for a public relations company.
Convoca comes from the verb 'convocar',
which basically means to 'call people
together'. The solution: a logo that shouts.

EVA VARGAS

Eva Vargas
Eva Vargas specializes in aquatic programmes for health, providing training, water workshops and tailor-made courses for fitness centres and sports facilities.

La Botiga
Re-design for La Botiga. The solution was to run the word Botiga over two lines, making a feature of BO (good, in Catalan) and carrying the idea through to La BOdega (wine cellar) and LavaBO (toilets!). Currently there are three *La Botiga* restaurants in Barcelona.

Fruit Yoghourts
The design task for these premium quality yoghourts centered around the communication of real fruit and a sense of creamy luxury.

UNA OBRA GASTRONÒMICA   DIRIGIDA PER
EL MAÎTRE
ESCRITA I PRODUÏDA PER
EL CUINER
AJUDANTS DE DIRECCIÓ
ELS CAMBRERS
INTÈRPRET PRINCIPAL
LA BONA CUINA
AMB LA PARTICIPACIÓ ESPECIAL DEL NOSTRE
GRAN PÚBLIC

La Tramoia
A popular bar and eatery on Rambla Catalunya, in the centre of Barcelona. The restaurant has a theatrical name, so I based the identity around a stage idea. The menu covers became a poster for a show starring the maître, the waiters and of course the cook, who takes the applause at the end.

Select Olives
A bold, striking design for a range of olive jars, each one containing olives from a particular region of Spain. The labels depict typical scenes from each of the regions: the Sant Climent de Taüll church in Catalonia, a classic Majorcan boat, and the windmills of Castilla-La Mancha...Don Quijote country!

espelmes
basicasa

vaixella
basicasa

plats
basicasa

basi©asa
coses per casa

  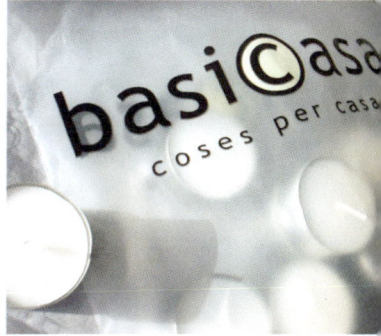

Basicasa
Identity for a shop selling reasonably priced household goods. The first part of the project was to devise a name. Different applications were designed around the letter C of the logo, the union letter between Basic and Casa (house).

Get Well Soon
I made this card for a relative who'd gone into hospital. I was in Menorca at the time and all that was available was some kraft paper and an old typewriter. I just turned the message into something that would help pass the time.

...HOPEFULLY YOU'LL BE BETTER
BEFORE YOU'VE EVEN STARTED!!!

P.S. THERE'S AT LEAST 62 WORDS!
SEE THE BACK PAGE

SOOT	NOW	LOT	EEL
SEEN	NOSE	LET	EWE
SEE	NEW	LOOT	
SWELL	NEWT	LONE	WOOL
STEEL	NO	LOO	WE
STEW		LEG	WET
SWELT	TWO	LOOSE	WENT
SLEET	TELL	LOSE	WON
SEG	TON	LOW	WEST
SON	TONE	LOG	
SOW	TOLL	LENS	ONE
SEW	TOOL		OWN
SOLE	TOWN	GEL	OWL
SWOT	TOW	GOT	
SNOW	TOE	GOOSE	
SLOW	TEN	GO	
	TOWEL	GONE	
NOTE	TOO	GOWN	
NOT	TO	GLEE	
NOOSE			
NEST			

Copyright Neil Cutler.

Panettone & Turrón

Panettone is a classic Italian Christmas dessert, popular in many countries, including Spain. What *Panettone* is to Italy, the *'Turrón'* is to Spain (opposite page).
These two projects for Eroski's Consumer label were done several years apart, but with a common brief, to produce a festive and desirable design.

Coffee & Cappuccino
Packs made into sacks! The design for this range of packaging aimed to capture the import/export essence of the coffee trade. Rich, dark colours and a hint of gold add quality to the line.
A vibrant, Art Deco-style illustration of Venice was commissioned for the Cappuccino pack, in reference to its Italian origins.

Reusable bag
I was briefed to design a reusable shopping bag for Eroski supermarkets. Eroski didn't want a bag that directly pushed environmental issues, rather one that people were happy to use on a daily basis. The solution uses nature photos in the form of coloured stripes to make an attractive, fashionable and above all unisex bag. A blue/green based bag was presented initially, but the client wanted a more corporate look, so the red version was released first. The bags were immensely popular. In summer the beaches were full of them and many were even spotted abroad.

Obvius
Obvius is a high quality London Dry Gin, pure and bright, and a minimalist approach to the design aims to convey this.

Martinez Bujanda Winery
Identity for a winery in La Rioja, the largest wine producing region of Spain. Created using six circles, the identity illustrates the four main phases of the production process, from grape picking to wine tasting.

Fundación Germina
The Germina Foundation is a nonprofit organization dedicated to providing opportunities for young people, with an emphasis on education and culture.
The foundation operates an after-school centre for underprivileged 6 to 12-year-olds.

MedCor
MedCor is one of the leading Spanish companies specializing in products used for heart surgery.

tueste

Caffriccio
COFFEE COMPANY

Caffriccio
Logo and visual identity for a new chain of cafés. The name was created from a combination of the words Cafe and Capricho (treat). The first *Caffriccio* opened in Madrid Airport's new Terminal 4, and is now present in other airports in Spain, Chile and Morocco.

HAPPY B

IRTHDAD!

Birthday Card
I was making a birthday card for my dad, typed too fast and accidentally typed a 'd' instead of a 'y'. I scrapped the original card I was making and went with the mistake.

Popcorn

The initial design I did for this range of packs was the volcano one, the 'Disaster movie'. Four years later I was asked to do two more packs, and decided to extend the film theme, adding the Sci-Fi adventure movie and the Western. Albert Rocarols helped me out on the new versions with two great little illustrations. The clapperboard/Pac-Man idea was a device used on the back of the packs.

Sand from the beach at Puerto Banús (only 5 minutes away)

Sand from one of our bunkers (we're surrounded by three nine hole golf courses)

La Quinta Golf Resort, Marbella
Several months prior to the event, the directors of the hotel wanted to announce the future opening of what would be a luxury golf hotel close to the beach. There were no photos of the hotel, which was in construction.
The solution: sand!

The sand we use in the construction of our hotel

The Westin La Quinta Golf Resort, Marbella
OPENING SEPTEMBER 2000

The Spanish
OPEN
28th April-1st May 2000

The European
OPEN
Hamburg 18th-21st May 2000

The US
OPEN
15th-18th June 2000

The British
OPEN
20th-23rd July 2000

The Italian
OPEN
26th-29th October 2000

The Westin La Quinta Golf Resort, Marbella
OPENING
3rd November 2000

OPEN

La Quinta Golf Resort, Marbella
I presented three designs for the invitation to the opening party of the hotel, all valid ideas: a waiter holding the drinks tray wearing a golfing glove, a rocket placed in the hole on the green (instead of the flag), and the chosen one, shown opposite.

Above: Christmas card sent out to clients and friends of the hotel.

Honey

Each of these honeys comes from one particular variety of flower. The label was designed to make the most of the hexagonal jars chosen, which reflect the shape of a honeycomb. German photographer Peter Toepfer took the photos for the labels. Aside from being a photographer and illustrator, Peter also just happens to be a beekeeper!

Corn Flakes
Corn Flakes are a classic cereal at the breakfast table, and the design aims to reflect this. Sunny, bright, bold and traditional, with a broad appeal.

Freezer Bag
Found next to the freezers in the supermarket, these bags are useful for getting your frozen shopping home still frozen. Worth a fun solution.

Flavoured Yoghourts
The brightly coloured illustrations of these fruit flavoured yoghourts aimed to make product identification easy and give the range maximum shelf impact.

...THEIR PATHS CROSS
VAL D'ISERE, 30 DECEMBER 1996...

...THE FIRST DATE
THE CINEMA, SUNDAY 2 FEBRUARY 1997...

...THE FIRST KISS
DINNER AT MAGGIE'S, FRIDAY 7 FEBRUARY 1997...

...THE WEDDING
OLIVELLA, SPAIN · SUNDAY 13 SEPTEMBER 1998
16.00H...

...LA FIESTA!
SANT PERE DE RIBES · SUNDAY 13 SEPTEMBER 1998
19.00H...

Wedding Invitations
I used a booklet story idea for both of these wedding invitations.
The one for Maggie and Michel tells the story of how they met when skiing, went to the cinema etc....

For Jorge and Katya I'd noticed that both their initials coincided in the alphabet, and from there came the title 'Love Letters' and the phrase 'Always Together'.

LOVE LETTERS

JORGE & KATYA   JK

ALMEIDA & BAUVAL   AB

ALWAYS TOGETHER

ABCDEFG
HIJKLMN
OPQRST
UVWXYZ

ON SATURDAY THE 28TH OF
SEPTEMBER 2002 AT 7.30PM
WE WILL BE CELEBRATING
OUR MARRIAGE AT THE
HACIENDA MORENO IN
ALHAURIN EL GRANDE
CLOSE TO MALAGA. SPAIN

Citrus
A leafy logo for a restaurant with a fruity name. A small oval sticker was designed, similar to the ones found on fruit, and this was applied to the menu covers, the daily dishes menu, invoices etc....

N
December
J

merry christmas from Neil and Jeannine

Christmas Cards
This card from 2003 is my favourite of the cards I designed for myself and my partner at the time, Jeannine.
Opposite page: card from my first Christmas in Barcelona.

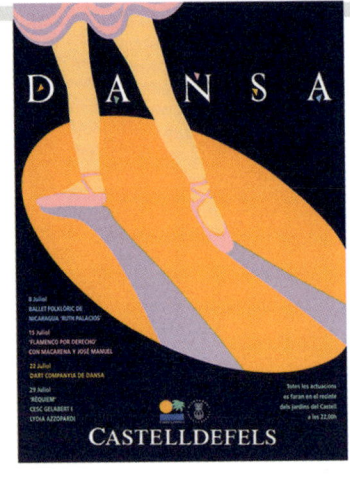

CASTELLDEFELS

CASTELLDEFELS

CASTELLDEFELS

CASTELLDEFELS

CASTELLDEFELS

CASTELLDEFELS

CASTELLDEFELS

CASTELLDEFELS

Castelldefels

Logo, identity and corporate manual designed to promote the beach resort of Castelldefels, clearly defining the Mediterranean character of the town. The poster advertising the dance festival was used for several years. Curiously, one of the designs I did during this project was eventually used (and still is) for the Barcelona Stock Exchange.

MundoSelecto

MundoSelecto is an online company specializing in bio and fair-trade food, including cereals, dried fruits and food supplements. Some interesting proposals were presented, and five different logo designs made the final cut. The MS leaf logo was the winner. With plans for a possible store opening in the future, the logo shown on the opposite page was also chosen.

Millenium
An exclusive line of packs, labels and collectable tins for high quality products, designed and produced to celebrate the millenium year. The main aim here was to find an attractive way to unify such a diverse range of premium products, some fifteen packs in all.
With the millennium year over, the line was adapted and continued under the banner 'Selección'.

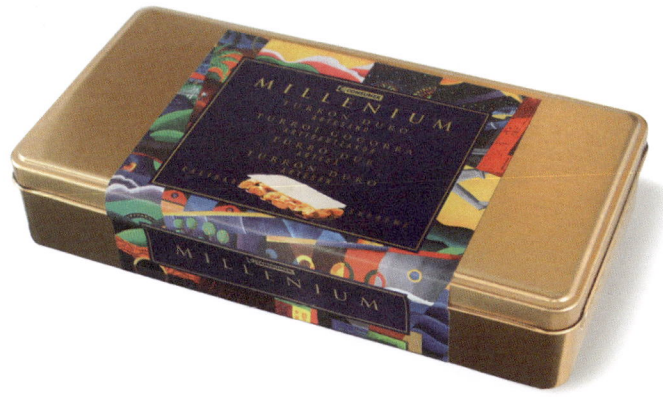

Café logo
This logo was part of one of the options presented during work on the Caffriccio project. In the end the identity took a different direction (see page 155), but I always liked this as a stand alone graphic symbol.

Follow the
Beijing Olympic Games
live in
BAR CENT ONZE

Le MERIDIEN
BARCELONA

Olympic Logo
Logo designed for a display, which was
positioned next to the reception desk of the hotel
Le Méridien during the 2008 Olympic Games.
The aim was to encourage hotel guests to watch
the event live in the hotel bar.

Nonell
Located in the Isidre Nonell square in Barcelona, the identity for Nonell is based around a leaf taken from one of the trees in front of the restaurant. A fresh and elegant look, combined with some fun applications.

Rejected...twice!

Rejected!
I was asked to design a Christmas card for a client that has several restaurants in Barcelona.
I came up with the idea of Christmas lights on a plate, a sort of 'Christmas light spaghetti' if you like, and a text along the lines of wishing people a year full of light and peace. This is the visual I presented, I was very happy with it. But the client not so. Let's just say they didn't see the light.
A few years later a book about rejected designs was published, and I was asked to send some work in for possible inclusion.
So I sent my rejected 'spaghetti' card in, thinking it would finally be published. It wasn't!

The design on the opposite page is the one that was eventually accepted by the client.
I was also happy with it. They too. So much so that they used it again the following year!

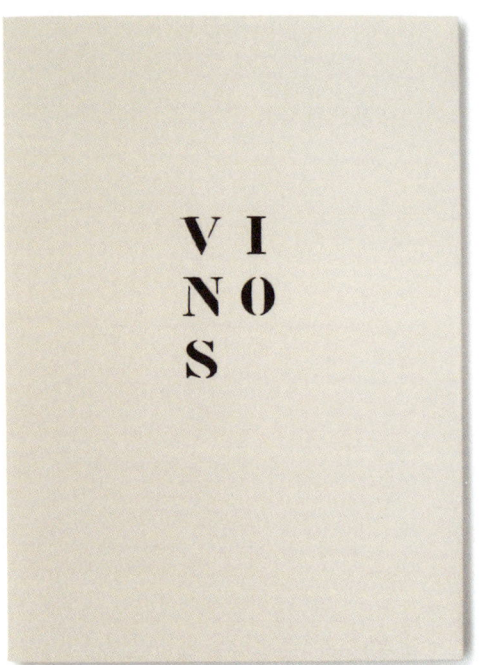

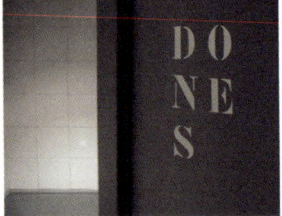

Sucoa
The name for this tapas restaurant is derived from that of its proprietor, Susana Conesa Acón. From there came the idea to arrange the letters in three lines, and from there the idea for the food and wine menus, and the signage for the toilets.

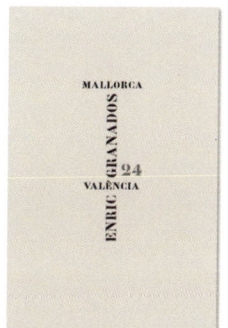

SU
CO
A

TAPAS &
PLATILLOS

THANKS

Thanks to all my clients, past and present (including the ones that aren't represented in this book) and to all the people who I've had the pleasure to work with over the years. Too many to mention, you all know who you are. Also to the marketing department of Grupo Eroski for their support and enthusiasm on many of the packaging projects shown.

To Sylvie, Beatriz and all the team at Index Book.

For their contributions to this book: Phil, Becky and Adriana at Delicooks, Jon, Inés, Meike and Barbara.

To all my family and friends, especially to Mireille for her love, patience and huge bowls of pasta! Also to Ritchie, Ian, Roger, Jon, Ian, David, Neil Finn and FC Barcelona for some great moments.

This book is dedicated to Millie, 101.

All the projects in this book were designed and art directed by Neil Cutler.

The Castelldefels identity and Repsol Christmas card were designed by Neil Cutler for Rolando & Memelsdorff. The Martínez Bujanda Winery identity was designed by Neil Cutler for CR Communication and Design Services. Thanks Carlos and Frank.

Thanks also to Carlos Martínez.

All logos illustrated by Neil Cutler. Illustrators and photographers who collaborated on some of the projects shown: Amanda Adams, Keith Adams, Carlos Andreu, Isabel Azcárate, John Forder, Becky Lawton, Manel Ortega, Tony Putman, Martin Rigo, Albert Rocarols, Jordi Sàbat, Philip Stanton, Peter Toepfer, Dany Virgili, Guillem Vergés.

Visiting Barcelona? Don't miss these two wonderful places on the Costa Brava, my favourites, Calella de Palafrugell and Cadaqués.

Left:
Some of the envelopes I've received over the years. I mean, one thing is being called Milk Cutler, or even Niv Draper, but Señorita?!....

HASTA PRONTO...